# LET YOUR VOICE SPEAK

## ROEBAIN

ISBN 979-888606988-4

# Contents

# Contents

# Contents

# Contents

# Preface

*The poems in her book consist mostly about her as a victim of abuse. She wants to use her book as a platform for her voice to be heard as it was silent for many years. Now she wants to encourage every woman to let her voice be heard don't be ashamed to tell your story as long as you keep quiet, you stay a victim and the abuser will continue with his malicious deeds.*

*The first poem she wrote is" I am a SLUT I wrote this poem as an irony for many women who are labled as a slut by partners, boyfriends or husbands. This book represents her freedom. Her voice speaks that she is no longer a victim but a victorious survivor.*

*This book will represent who I am. "I am the book and the book is me.*

# About The Author

*Roebain*

She is a single mom of two and also an educator. Who loves nature and seized every opportunity in the outdoors. She was born on 25 August 1970 during the apartheid laws.

As a South African she started to fight in her teenage years for human rights. Roebain started to write in June 2020, when a stranger saw a picture of her on Facebook and wrote a poem about her. Since then she fell in love with poetry and never looked back. She received many awards in 2020 for her poems. She also became the South African ambassador for Oxygen Pen and host on OPT LIT. she is also appointed as a regional manager for Africa Ambassadors. As a humanitarian and empath, one of her dreams is to be a motivational speaker against women and child abuse.

Awards she received from different poetry sites were: Certificates for excellent achievements, Honourable mentions, Poet of the day, Poet of the week, Poet of the Month, Certificate of Excellence in motivational writing Topmost engaged member, Poet of the Year. Roebain also interviewed well-known writers across the globe.

# Acknowledgements

*First and most important I would like to thank my God who gives me the inspiration, courage, and wisdom to write. He put me back together. Without Him, I will surely fail in my mission to accomplish my journey and reach my destiny.*

*I wish to convey my deepest gratitude to my special friend, Mark. I am greatly indebted for his inspiring tutelage, guidance, compassion, patience, and unremitting care and support in terms of my ambition. His poem "Roebain the rose" inspired me to fall in love with poetry. He saw my talent and let me embrace it. He is not only my friend but my mentor.*

*I also wish to express my sincere thanks and gratitude to:*

*My children (Randy and Marshé) I love so much. You were always fighting my battles with me since a young age and continue to inspire me and help me move forward. I am so glad I have two angels walking beside me.*

*Ankit who made it possible. He is a very dear friend who went*

*beyond his duty to make my dream possible.*

*And lastly, I like to thank all my readers, family, and friends who encourage me.*

*I, Roebain wish to convey my deepest gratitude to World of Soul publications, for making my dream a reality. I am honored that you accepted my work to be published under your name.*

*I am impressed with your professionalism and work ethos. I hope in the future you render your service again and we will have a good partnership between client and service provider.*

*By saying this I am humbled and blessed to have a prestigious company that published my first book. Thank you. Roebain*

# 1. I Rise

*From victim to survivor, I rise,*
*I fell, I got*
*From under on Top.*
*From slave to the boss.*
*I am the queen of my castle.*
*You thought you would break me,*
*But here I am today.*
*Better than before.*
*I rise,*
*I won the war.*
*I rise, I rise,*
*Above it All.*
*From victim to Survivor.*
*I rise,*
*I am the queen of my castle.*

# 2. A Light will kill the Pain

*How my soul is yearning,*
*For someone to come to rescue me,*
*From the turmoil a prison of hell.*
*I pray and call out, To Your name.*
*Please, Lord, Take this cup away.*
*When darkness fell upon me,*
*I trembled with fear.*
*Will, it be my last night,*
*With the terror and pain?*
*I learn to block it out.*
*Feel no more pain.*
*My body was bruised and beaten.*
*I locked myself up in my brain.*
*Hold on, I whispered to myself*
*Hold on, the darkness will pass.*
*A new day is coming.*
*A light will kill the pain.*

# 3. Alone

*When my loneliness stalks me,*
*I am a hermit in a world with many souls and faces.*
*No one to talk to, share my dreams and desires,*
*No one to inspire.*
*I wish I am still a child to play in the sand,*
*And make new friends.*
*O dread is the day, I feel so astray.*
*No one to share how I feel inside,*
*All my feelings I must hide.*
*I wish, sometimes I was still a child,*
*I can play on my own,*
*I won't feel so alone.*
*Why is there no one for me?*
*To hug, love, and watch the last sun rays of the day.*
*That will make me feel ok.*
*This feeling embitters my soul,*
*I want to feel whole.*
*I wish, that there is someone out there,*
*Whom my loneliness I can share.*

# 4. Betrayed by a friend

*Let me tell you my story, I hope it's not boring,*
*It started with a friend request,*
*My intuition told me not to invest.*
*Her friendship was fake, I made a huge mistake.*
*With an angel face and sweet endearments,*
*She camouflaged her procurement.*
*She infiltrated my circle, portrait to be kind,*
*All along she had a devious mind.*
*Becoming my friend,*
*I should have known it was not Godsend.*
*She stung her poison deep into his soul.*
*He lost all control.*
*Caught up in her web, he sunk deep in her trap.*
*Their affair spiral out of control.*
*She swallowed him whole.*
*He was lost, no more mine, nowhere to be found.*
*The betrayal was so deep, help I had to seek.*
*To make sure this will never happen again,*
*I prefer not to make friends.*
*That moment changed everything.*
*For me as a human being.*

# 5. Circle of LIFE

*The circle of Life is a mystery on its own,*
*It teaches me where I do not belong.*
*You see, it intrigues me, to be faithful to my course,*
*And have no remorse.*
*My life is a reflection of my mother.*
*It was like reliving it in a mirror.*
*With all its terror.*
*She endures the suffering of an unfaithful husbands' abuse,*
*And his low self-esteem as an excuse.*
*She fought all her battles with might.*
*And still, l try to do what was right.*
*Through all her pain and misfortunes she has to bare,*
*She stood firm and fair.*
*Life treated her bad in many ways.*
*She cried most of her days.*
*But one day suddenly, she was set free,*
*To have a new life eternally.*
*Then my journey began, and believe me when I tell you it was not fun.*
*Hell was upon me, I live the same life as my mother you see,*
*An unfaithful and abusive husband.*
*Enduring suffering and pain,*
*There was just nothing in my marriage I could gain.*
*The circle of Life is a mystery, you will see.*
*You are the only one who can set you FREE.*

# 6. Come Soar with me

*When it was quiet and dark I was drowning in despair.*
*My sorrows were too deep,*
*For me alone to bear.*
*I called out your name,*
*Please, I need you now.*
*I will surrender.*
*This pain is tearing through flesh and bone.*
*I am so alone.*
*You lifted me up,*
*And took me to the highest mountain.*
*Where you took my hand, and soar with me.*
*High above the clouds,*
*Higher than my sorrows.*
*I soar with You,*
*Above all my despair*

# 7. Dauntless

*It took every fiber in her being,*
*Away from the horrific scene.*
*To stood there,*
*She hopes the court will be fair.*
*Answer all these questions, when, why, how,*
*Felt like an owl.*
*Repeating herself.*
*When in her past they started to dwell.*
*It happened so fast,*
*All she could remember was the blast.*
*Goliath was in front of the door.*
*Blocked her way, before she hit the floor.*
*She called on all her courage to face the ordeal.*
*Conjured David in her to appear.*
*Her dauntlessness grab the gun.*
*In a spun a new nightmare began.*
*The Headlines of the day.*
*Courageous was she, valor received!*

# 8. DEPRESSION

*Do you know how depression feels?*
*You are at the bottom of a hole with the vision of a mole.*
*No hate, or love,*
*You reach out for God from above.*
*You hear encouraging words all around you,*
*That makes no sense because your feelings are too dense.*
*You tried to grasp what they said but you just want to stay in bed.*
*Darkness fell upon you, day and night,*
*All you do is try, try to fight.*
*You know your way to reach for above so that you can feel the love.*
*But all in vain because your thoughts are insane.*
*Blackness descends on you, it is all around and keeps you bound.*
*Fighting your way to the top, it's now or never,*
*You know you can't stop.*
*This hell you are in, you must try to win.*
*An empty feeling inside, you try to hide, Away from friends and family.*
*That they must not see what you become, your feelings are numb.*
*A loss of appetite and energy.*
*Is the new way of living, while inside you are busy dying.*
*You fool yourself to say you will be ok, you try harder, Depression is not going to make you are a martyr.*
*Fighting to stay alive, you seek help in a clinic,*
*So that your kids can stop panicking.*
*It drains you to see them suffer, because of you,*

*And there is nothing you can do.*
*Do you know what depression is?*
*It is a dangerous beast.*

# 9. Do you HEAR me?

You supposed to protect me,
From your beloved son.
When I run with an outcry,
"He's behind me with a gun."
Do you hear me, do you see my blood,
Running down my face?
Or is my life not worth,
For your precious family name to be put in disgrace?
Naked, I stood before you,
Pleading you for help.
But you turned a blind eye,
While he brought down the belt.
Do you hear me?
Do you see the blood?
Running down my face?
Instead, you worried about your precious reputation that will be a
disgrace.

# 10. Eden

*In the Garden of Eden, there they were, Adam and Eve.*
*Until they were deceived.*
*Everyone thinks it was a snake,*
*But that is our biggest mistake.*
*He was a handsome, wicked dark knight,*
*Radiant once with a bright light.*
*He stroked his revenge with might.*
*He wanted to punish Gods' creation,*
*So he used his demonization.*
*Because of his betrayal, we were cursed,*
*The consequences for sinful actions,*
*Was nakedness and rejection.*
*We all believe it was an apple,*
*That made Eve rattle.*
*What if he deceived her with human flesh?*
*That's why we are now in such a mess.*
*Adam wants a piece of the pie,*
*So Eve decided they must lie.*
*Cain and Abel were born,*
*One from good and one from evil spawn.*
*In the garden, there, they were no more,*
*Behind them, God closes the door.*
*The Garden of Eden was closed, for heaven and earth,*
*And open the door for a new generations' birth.*

# 11. Fatal Attraction

*Let us call a spade a spade,*

*You are making feeble excuses for your mistakes.*

*My respect you must earn,*

*All the trust between us you have burned.*

*Playing Russian roulette with my feelings,*

*I am sick and tired of your mistreatment.*

*Your feelings are like a roller coaster every day,*

*I think you are just obsessed with me anyway.*

*I am done with your insecurities,*

*Tell me, you love me?*

*That is just your game, misleading me.*

*Every time we are supposed to go on a date,*

*You have to work late.*

*On weekends you are never free,*

*To spend time with me.*

*There is always something that you have to do,*

*Then you blamed me for not having time for you?*

*Are you kidding me, to think?*

*I am so irresponsible, to let you in?*

*Break down my walls.*

*I built them especially for men like you,*

*Who wants to make women feel small.*

# 12. Forget me

*Hi, it is time that I must tell you,*
*Forget that I told you, I love you,*
*It was all a lie.*
*Forget that I show you how I feel,*
*It was not real.*
*Forget all the messages, I send you,*
*It was not true.*
*Forget that special moment we laughed and cried,*
*Say goodbye to them.*
*Forget my photo in your frame,*
*It is not me, but a picture from a magazine.*
*Forget that I exist,*
*I am just another woman on your list.*
*Forget the letter I send, burn it in the fire,*
*Your time with me has Expire!*

# 13. Give me a Voice to flicker

*I like to tell my story, painting my words with poetry.*
*Silent was my voice for so long,*
*At last, I know where I belong.*
*Please, don't dim my light,*
*When it just started to flicker brightly.*
*For so long I live in fear,*
*No voice that someone can hear.*
*Many nights I want to scream,*
*To wake up from this nightmare that was not a dream.*
*Using words to tell my story of abuse is my victory.*
*A genius I am not, I only learn how, now, to express me,*
*Because my words were kept in a cell,*
*In a prison of hell.*
*These words I write, to you,*
*It makes me feel brand new.*
*With them, I can paint my canvas,*
*And let the ink flow in its rows.*
*All I want to do is to encourage others like me,*
*You can also be free.*
*No one can take away, the power of your words,*
*It is yours and mine, so let us shine.*

# 14. Holding Back my Tears

*Who needs an enemy?*

*If I had a friend like you.*

*I wish the lines above were not true.*

*We are not at Primary school,*

*Where I was your fool.*

*Always pushing me to the back,*

*As long as you could be,*

*The teacher's pet.*

*You have everything good,*

*Do you have to steal mine too?*

*I thought we are back to friendship.*

*Catching up.*

*Our broken past, we are busy mending.*

*But you were so sly.*

*Hiding your true intentions.*

*Nowhere in our conversations,*

*I picked up your devious plan.*

*Until I saw what you have done.*

*Enjoy it while it lasts.*

*Your sins of the past, will haunt you.*

*It took me years,*

*To build my self-esteem, what you and others do, I redeem.*

*Holding back my tears, I will overcome it.*

# 15. I am a SLUT

*Cuddle in a bundle*
*I lay down in my blood.*
*Soaking wet with tears I wish I was dead.*
*Not yet, my child, You said.*
*Not yet your time is up.*
*Be strong, and fight the battle,*
*Because a war must still be won.*
*Draining and exhausted.*
*From the beatings,*
*I called out Your name.*
*My throat was sore of all the choking, I whisper, please help!*
*You gave me the strength,*
*You gave me the courage to pick myself up.*
*And here I am today, Your SLUT.*
*Strong, Liberated, Unique, and Tough*

# 16. I am death

*You asked me, Death, where is your sting?*
*Well to your family and friends the pain I bring.*
*Whose fault is that?*
*When I took your last breath.*
*Many bodies I put to rest,*
*And their faith was put to the test.*
*Now their bones laid in a shallow grave,*
*Hoped their souls would be safe.*
*You challenged me,*
*Created viruses in a laboratory.*
*You are always at war,*
*Want to be rich and ashamed to be poor.*
*You created your own destruction,*
*Substances abused, nature polluted,*
*I think you all are confused thinking,*
*I play by your rules.*
*You caused your own tragedies,*
*I only took you out, your miseries.*
*You welcomed me into your house,*
*Begged to take your friends, even your spouse.*
*Now you cry, don't want to say goodbye?*
*It is too late you have to live with your mistakes.*
*I will always be around,*
*A new body to be found.*

*That is my sting, heartaches I bring.*

# 17. I shall not want

*He leads me through valleys,*
*Away from the dangerous rallies.*
*I shall not want.*
*My cup overflows with blessings,*
*Although my faith has been tested.*
*I shall not want. In pastures green,*
*He leads me down,*
*Although a spiritual war is all around,*
*I shall not want.*
*He protects me with a rod and staff,*
*When things are really tough.*
*I shall not want.*
*Our Israel does not sleep nor slumber,*
*Even when the enemy attacks us in numbers.*
*I shall not want.*
*In His house, the table is laid,*
*For us, our sins are paid.*
*I shall not want.*
*The Lord is my shepherd.*
*I shall not want.*

# 18. It is Time

*Why are people so disturbed?*
*From all the unholy news they heard.*
*These are God's proclamations,*
*It is in Revelation.*
*Nation against nation,*
*Mothers will cry for all their babies that died.*
*One will stand, ten thousand will fall,*
*The writing is on the wall.*
*It is time to take a stand,*
*We all will play in a one-man-band.*
*But don't fret, because it's not all gloom,*
*We are not doomed.*
*He is coming soon to bring redemption,*
*Ending all these devastations.*
*You have to decide where your alliance will be,*
*With the Son or enemy?*
*Before He comes for retribution,*
*Salvation is your solution.*
*Shed your old skin, repent before the cross,*
*And your soul will not be lost.*
*It is time to take a stand,*
*Before the world will end.*

# 19. It is my Time

*It's my Time to reign in my domain.*
*Stand back haters, and betrayers.*
*It's my time, at last, you treated me as an outcast,*
*I am free from you, you stay in my past.*
*I step into my light, it is shining bright.*
*I claim a life of abundance, your jealousy is so redundant.*
*For many years, I was in your shadows, making myself small,*
*So that all of you can stand tall.*
*I took the wrap for your mistakes,*
*Keep quiet, when you speak hate.*
*You never gave me a chance, to explain my side of the story,*
*Instead, you claim all the glory.*
*Stand back haters, and betrayers,*
*It's my time to shine and reign.*
*You are now in my domain.*
*At last, I am free from your captivity.*
*I can now be true to myself,*
*I escaped the prison of hell.*
*It is my Time.*

# 20. Keep me alive

*It is still in the darkness,*
*With a pillow on my head.*
*Suffocating without breath,*
*I can smell the alcohol on my neck.*
*He sits on top of me,*
*Beating me to death.*
*Please, Lord, spare my life,*
*My kids still need me,*
*Let me live another day.*
*I grab unto the bedsheets,*
*While he rains the pain on me,*
*I know that one day I'll be free.*
*When he is done doing,*
*What he does best.*
*I'll creep out softly,*
*To lay on the floor to rest.*
*Tomorrow is a new day,*
*To start fresh.*

# 21. Let me sleep

*I just want to sleep a little bit longer,*
*So that I can feel stronger.*
*I just want to rest before the beast's conquest.*
*He ravaged my body last night,*
*Choked me with an electrical cord,*
*While hitting me with the iron board.*
*Please, let me just close my eyes and sleep,*
*I want to escape his hell, don't weep.*
*Banged my head against the wall,*
*Struck me with his fist I fall.*
*Lying here in my blood,*
*I want to escape from this thug.*
*I want to sleep a little bit longer,*
*So I can be stronger tomorrow.*
*I will fight with all his demons,*
*Speak life over my soul and break his control.*
*So let me sleep, please, do not weep.*
*One day I will be free and live happily*

# 22. The Purged

*Liberated and confident she stood there,*
*Embracing the moonlight and fresh air.*
*Tears softly ran down her cheeks.*
*Usually anxiously, waiting for his text,*
*Standing here, let her feel relaxed.*
*Spontaneously she started to laugh out loud,*
*People must wonder who is so silly in the crowd?*
*Relief from all the stress and pain,*
*Every single moment she decided, will not be in vain.*
*Adventurous days, are waiting for her,*
*Determined she will adhere.*
*Leaving him was the best thing she could do,*
*Oblivious, was he to think she will not too.*
*Valedictory and bon voyage is hers,*
*Ever ready for new Love to occur.*

# 23. Mirror, mirror on the wall

*Mirror, mirror on the wall,*
*Please tell me who is the real me of them all?*
*Is she the girl who dreamt of her knight in shining armor and a happy*
*ever after?*
*Or the one who was a victim of abuse, and survived?*
*Fought her way to stay alive.*
*Perhaps the divorced, single mum,*
*Who struggles on her own?*
*Breaking flesh and bone to build herself a home?*
*Maybe the visionary teacher,*
*Who wants her kids to succeed?*
*Even if she had to ignore her own needs.*
*Can you give her a clear explanation?*
*Where she is heading to, and her destination?*
*The uncertainty drives her mad,*
*Especially when she is alone and has no one to phone.*
*No lover, to warm her bed,*
*No companion, to rest her head.*
*No confidant, to share her fears,*
*No one, to dry her tears.*
*When you look at her reflection,*
*Do you also see her imperfections?*
*Can you see her broken soul?*
*That she tries to make whole.*

*What about all the rejections,*
*Can you fix her with an injection?*
*Mirror, mirror on the wall,*
*Is she just not also human after all?*

# 24. My Poker face

*I know you judge me,*
*But if you only know.*
*How much I have to pretend*
*You will understand.*
*High collars, long sleeves,*
*And pants even if it's hot.*
*You ask me, if I am silly,*
*Or just a lady with a different fashion style.*
*If you only know me, you will understand,*
*How much I have to pretend.*
*You think I am too serious,*
*Not laughing for your jokes.*
*It will hurt to laugh,*
*Where my rib case are beaten to a pulp.*
*If you only know me, you will understand,*
*How much I have to pretend.*

# 25. My visitor

*In a dream, he came to me,*

*Told me, there were visions I had to see.*

*On the peak of the mountain, waited near the fountain.*

*Majestic, he stood,*

*With a halo above his hair.*

*Bright brown eyes,*

*That will never tell lies.*

*Dressed in shining armor,*

*I could feel his power.*

*He told me his name is Daniel,*

*I must take off my sandals.*

*On the holy ground, I tread,*

*A new beginning lays ahead.*

*When I wake up, I could still sense, His presence.*

# 26. The wolf

*When I was a child,*
*I dreamt of white picket fences.*
*And cuddling on a coach.*
*Long walks on a beach,*
*And hot chocolate on a winter's night.*
*Instead three months into the marriage.*
*I was welcome with a fist.*
*My dreams were shattered into nightmares of horrors and pain,*
*My hopes were blowing up in vain.*
*Although life was growing inside me.*
*It did not stop the pain.*
*More beatings and humiliation, leads to lies, to family, doctors, and*
*friends.*
*How long must I keep on?*
*Or my walls will be crumbling down.*
*My wolf is not outside my house,*
*That blows my house down.*
*He lied his way inside,*
*And broke my guard down.*
*Like a pig prepared for slaughter,*
*He broke me piece by piece down.*
*His howls were just as worst as bites,*
*He brought his wrath down with might.*
*Can someone please come to rescue me?*

*From the big bad wolf,*
*Whose huffs and puffs,*
*Blow me down.*

# 27. Tears

*Laying down on my bed to rest,*
*A flood of emotions ran through my head.*
*Tears rolled down my face,*
*For Your love and grace.*
*As I cried I want to say, thank you, Lord, for all the pain,*
*These lessons I learned were not in vain.*
*Tears, for all the people who crossed my path,*
*The good and bad, those who made me happy and sad.*
*I wondered if it was me, who is abnormal in society,*
*No longer want to be in the circle of popularity?*
*I am tired of chasing after the wind,*
*Just to earn an extra few shillings.*
*Life is more than wasting time on vanity.*
*Tears, for all my blessings, my kids and home,*
*For Your firstborn love has no beginning or end,*
*To all, You are a best friend.*

# 28. The empty seat

*Every day I had to beg and plea,*
*For him to take his seat.*
*He rather preferred to take the broom,*
*And sweep the room.*
*No, interest in Maths or English,*
*For him, it was all gibberish.*
*Creative Arts, makes him smile,*
*He can draw and perform all day long.*
*On Monday morning, I got a surprise.*
*He waited for me, took the key,*
*Today no begs or pleas.*
*The whole week, no fidgeting,*
*But very inquisitive.*
*How, when, he exclaims.*
*Very seriously, it made me curious.*
*On Friday afternoon,*
*When everybody said goodbye,*
*He turned and smiled.*
*On Monday morning, I received the news,*
*He went with friends to the beach.*
*An accident occurred,*
*And everything went blurry.*
*His seat stays empty.*

# 29. The Stand

*There they stand on no men's land, two knights,*
*One from the dark, one from the light.*
*Face to face, they started their race, conjured a human war.*
*Dark knight: He strikes with all his might,*
*Used Bible verses, cruel curses and Blasphemy unto Thee.*
*Offered Him a world of splendor,*
*In return, He must renounce His sender.*
*Light Knight: His reply to the vendor was,*
*All this splendor belongs not to him but to the one and only King.*
*He who not seek the glory of His Father,*
*Is nor His sister or His brother.*
*Dark Knight: Got so angry and fierce, He calls upon his soldiers.*
*To take the knight to be crucified, hang Him 'till He dies.*
*Light Knight: He just smiles, because He knows He must die.*
*To offer Himself for salvation, was years ago a proclamation.*
*Dark Knight: On Good Friday he celebrated his victory,*
*His enemy hung on Calvary. He thought he won the war,*
*He's the one the world must adore.*
*Light Knight: On the third day the Earth gave away,*
*He rose from the grave and locked the dark knight in a cave*
*The victory was His, and to all who want to receive.*
*His glory to live eternally.*

# 30. Twin Flames

*Nostalgia is creeping up on me,*
*Walking back into history.*
*Back then, we were only nine,*
*There's no way we knew we ran out of time.*
*I remembered our days in the park,*
*We played late, until dark.*
*You were me, and I were you,*
*Both wearing our red shoes.*
*You knew immediately what was wrong, with me,*
*Whispered sweet encouraging words in my ear,*
*Only for me to hear.*
*What happened then?*
*Why are we no longer friends?*
*Are you still angry, that I had to grow up fast?*
*Left you in my past.*
*I wished I could go back in time,*
*When we were both nine.*
*This time I'll take your hand,*
*So that you can walk with me into Neverland.*
*We would stay there as kids,*
*Playing carefree, eating sweet treats.*
*I am sorry I left you behind,*
*But it is better to remain nine.*

# 31. Vision

*You hold my hands,*
*Lifting me up.*
*Spinning me around, like*
*Your child.*
*I see your face, peaceful and filled with LOVE.*
*You walk beside me on the wet sand,*
*Covered with white light.*
*Come, you said, rest*
*Come, you said, be still.*
*We sit down, you, me, and all the creatures of the world.*
*Listen to Your voice.*
*Come, You said to rest,*
*Come, You said to be still.*
*Was it my imagination?*
*Or was it a Vision?*

# 32. WHY?

*All the questions in my head, making me mad.*

*You treated me as the enemy ever since, I married into your family.*

*All I want was, your approval to accept me as I am,*

*But the moment I stepped into your house I was damned.*

*Not knowing what I do is right or wrong,*

*Because you already decided I do not belong.*

*I was so used to your rejections, without any affections.*

*It broke my spirit down,*

*And many nights in my tears I will drown.*

*You darned make sure I got the message how you feel,*

*Just in case I thought it was not real.*

*Punishing me, by ignoring my children, when they seek your favor,*

*In return, you gave them bad behavior.*

*No one of you come to our rescue,*

*When your son sold my house and left us on the street,*

*Where I have to struggle to land on my feet.*

*I have so many questions in my head,*

*That makes me furious and you are oblivious.*

*I try to understand why people like you, can be so heartless and careless.*

*You played the judge and jury, when it comes to your sons' fury,*

*You believed all his lies, even when I almost died.*

*I stop wondering why,*

*What you did to me, because I am now free.*

*Free from you all, no beatings of my head against a wall.*

*I hope and pray that you will realize one day what you have done.*
*You will live with regrets and hate, and that will be your fate.*

• 37 •

# 33. I say

*They say, beware of a woman's scorn.*
*But I don't have to wait for revenge for long.*
*Karma will attack,*
*If I were you, I would watch my back.*
*You live very comfortably,*
*While I have to raise our kids alone.*
*Have a great life as an absent father.*
*Don't even bother, to wish your son a happy birthday.*
*Too busy playing the dutiful husband, to your 20 year younger wife.*
*They say, what goes around comes around.*
*Soon you will found, yourself old and grey.*
*Alone on your dying bed you will lay.*
*They say, what goes up must come down.*
*You thinking, you are standing tall?*
*Want me to feel small.*
*Stole my house and even the fridge.*
*What a leech.*
*But as the hands of time is ticking on,*
*So will your time end for all your wrongs.*
*They say, you can't build your happiness on someone else's pain.*
*That is exactly what both of you have done.*
*But remember on the long run, you two will get what you deserved,*
*The wheel will reverse*
*They say, you must forgive and forget.*

*But I only forgive those who deserves my respect.*
*For you, I don't have any,*
*Not for the pain and hurt you caused.*
*And still have no remorse.*
*They say, time heals everything, And Amen to it.*
*I say, good riddance of bad rubbish.*

# 34. My Abiding Home

*When I die, please don't cry.*

*I know where I go,*

*In a vision it was shown.*

*Open arms He will wait for me, I can't wait to embrace Him.*

*When I look up unto His face,*

*All I will see is His love and grace.*

*A new garment I will wear,*

*No more pain and sorrows to bare.*

*The angels will prepare a feast,*

*To celebrate the return of an earthly deceased.*

*In heaven I will be reborn, amongst the heavenly beings I now belong.*

*A cake with one candle I will blow,*

*To commemorate my one day, birthday and eternity days in a row.*

*So when I die, please don't cry.*

*Don't visit a shallow grave,*

*My bones are there but my soul is safe.*

# 35. My Journey my Life

*Memorable memories of my life I have, some are good and some are bad.*
*Young and innocent I was, that was a great memoir of my past.*
*Joyfully as a prankster back then, I had so many friends.*
*Ordinary mundane life was boring, I was an adrenaline junky.*
*Underdog of my siblings, I was not welcome in their company.*
*Relationships with my friends were ok for me, they were my family.*
*Never a dull day in my life, every opportunity was extraordinary.*
*Exceptional scholar at school, although some teachers I took for a fool.*
*Young and restless years were great then I made the worst mistake.*
*Married at a young age and endured every time a husband raged.*
*Yearning, back for my carefree life, especially when I thought I would not survive.*
*Life threw many curve balls at me, most of the time I was unhappy.*
*Independency was gone, I was married to an evil spawn.*
*Fight or flight I had to choose, or my life I would lose*
*Eureka!! I built a new life for myself, I am happy at least.*

# 36. No frills or curls

*If you expected an encyclopaedia from me,*
*Then you must live eternally.*
*I choose simplicity in my poetry.*
*My readers must understand,*
*And don't need to keep a dictionary at hand.*
*The messages that I convey,*
*Is my personality I portrays.*
*No fancy frills or curls,*
*Like some Barbie girls.*
*Only simple words that I speak,*
*The emotions from inside,*
*For years it hid.*
*It is ok if you comment or like, I will not bite.*
*My poems are for those,*
*Who feel the need to be inspire,*
*Their inspirational desires.*

# 37. Question

*I have a question for all the poets and poetess,*
*How do you know the grammar of your poem is right,*
*and mine is wrong?*
*When do I write in my home language that I was born?*
*I am South African, you Italian or maybe American.*
*I write and speak in a different way,*
*Not always how you would say.*
*But does it make my grammar right and yours wrong?*
*We all write down our emotions, dreams, and fears,*
*Is that not more important here?*
*I like painting my emotions on your poetry wall,*
*It makes me feel good to display them all.*
*So please, give me a break,*
*Even if you think I make grammar mistakes.*

# 38. She

*She is just a butterfly,*
*A creature of the sky.*
*Soaring high,*
*Seven days before she dies.*
*Wrap up in a cocoon,*
*She fought her way to bloom.*
*It took her months to portray her beauty,*
*All creatures envy.*
*Parading her delicate wings,*
*More precious than the treasures of kings.*
*Her colors reflect the rainbow,*
*On a petal, she loves to show.*
*Fly high, my butterfly,*
*Fly high, before you die.*
*Enjoy the splendor of Gods' creation,*
*That most mundane left in devastation.*

# 39. Single Mom

*I am both parents to my kids,*
*Sometimes I wish I was a witch.*
*I would create a spell,*
*To give unfaithful husbands hell.*
*Deliberately they broke their vowels,*
*And now you are a single spouse.*
*Day and night you have to wonder,*
*Do you fulfill their needs as a mother?*
*Because you don't want to neglect them as their father.*
*Juggling your life between work and a house,*
*There is no time for pleasures to feel aroused.*
*You are the caregiver, the provider, the mother, and father,*
*Instead of going on a date,*
*You prefer to sleep in late.*
*Exhausted and sometimes drain,*
*You hope all your efforts are not in vain.*
*Your kids will appreciate what you do,*
*And in return just love you.*

# 40. Sweet Memories

*Christmas time was the best memory under the pine tree.*
*In South Africa, we do not have a snowman and reindeers,*
*Instead, we celebrated it with cookies and ginger beer.*
*Days before Christmas we will make wreaths,*
*Out of cinnamon cookies and sweet treats.*
*Passing houses in the street, you will hear Bonnie M,*
*Singing on the beat of the drummer boy I will stomp my feet.*
*Baking cookies with mum, I had so much fun.*
*Three days before Christmas Eve, we will decorate our pine tree.*
*A star will be put on top that was always my job.*
*On Christmas Eve we will dress up, and wait till midnight for the ticky*
*band with a 5 cent in our hand.*
*All dress up in black and white,*
*They will sing O Holy Night.*
*And under the tree, we will end with Silent Night.*
*The night won't stop there, because presents must still be shared.*
*You cannot wait till they call your name,*
*Presents were a week before on your brain.*
*I received a red, plastic dialing phone,*
*The first toy I could call my own.*
*Christmas under the tree, Was my sweet memory.S*

# 41. The adventures of Life

*I am just a gypsy passing through,*

*Minding my own business, how about you?*

*Sitting here, listening to your poor souls,*

*How you were abused and used.*

*It is not adventurous at all, I experienced them all.*

*You took me too many places.*

*I just have to look at the expressions on your faces.*

*There is a happy place, Oh, she is full of grace.*

*Her eyes sparkle when it is her turn to tell her story,*

*Even if everybody else thinks it is boring.*

*Then there is the fierce, angry one,*

*Whose husband had an affair and now she is here to share.*

*How she wasted all her years, being his wife,*

*She could have a better life.*

*Listening to your stories and expressions on your faces,*

*I go to many adventurous places.*

*Where you have and what you become,*

*It makes me feel numb.*

*We do not experience glamorous days, like others always.*

*They go to exotic places, white sand beaches,*

*And eating sweet delicious peaches.*

*We are here, experiencing our journey,*

*Sharing stories, some are sad and some are boring.*

*But at least, we can collaborate, how it feels to have an adventurous life,*

*Even if it is not what we want.*

# 42. Be Yourself

*Stay grounded.*
*Focus on what you believe.*
*Hold on to integrity.*
*Be true to yourself.*
*Don't let their insecurities,*
*Derailed your course.*
*People who bully, have low self-esteem.*
*Be brave.*
*Show them who you are.*
*The world can be a war zone,*
*And people will do you wrong.*
*Empaths suffer the most.*
*Because they are the first to help.*
*They have honor,*
*And are profound.*

# 43. Believe in Your Dreams

*Become anyone you want to be all you have to do is believe.*
*Every person has a dream, but it's up to you if you want to reach for it.*
*Let no one tell you, you cannot become a doctor or astronaut.*
*It's in your hands what you will do, to make this dream come true. Efforts*
*and hard work will cost, maybe you have to work for a terrible boss.*
*Vacant thoughts and no efforts, and your dream will be lost.*
*Ensured you make your dream a reality, believe in possibilities.*
*Ingenuity must be your reality, for you not to be ordinary.*
*Never say I cannot or will try, then you can kiss your dream goodbye.*
*You have to believe in yourself, to make your dream come true. Obviously,*
*you cannot expect your dream to fall into your lap.*
*Use all the resources you can get, to make sure everything you do is perfect.*
*Rest, sometimes to get a new or fresh perspective, especially if you feel*
*rejected.*
*Do not give up, get up!*
*Rise above your storms, it will not be long, then you feel mighty and*
*strong.*
*Even if you feel not you cannot conquer all your obstacles, trust in*
*miracles.*
*Appreciate the small accomplishments, it brings you closer to bigger*
*achievement*
*Master your thoughts not to think negative, but always to think positive*
*Stars shine brighter at night, so be your own light, remember if you can*
*dream it, you can achieve it*

# 44. The revenged

*Andromeda was a beautiful queen.*
*She was very in love.*
*Now she is consumed with hate. She found out her lover is fake.*
*To betray her was his biggest mistake.*
*He didn't love her,*
*But her wealth and beauty.*
*Parading with her at parties,*
*Bragging about her dowries.*
*She wanted a man who do not fucked her over.*
*But someone who fought with her.*
*She concocted a plan, dressed up as a man.*
*She went to his nightclub,*
*To find out if it is true.*
*That with other women he screws.*
*She drew her gun, and shoot between his eyes,*
*For he deserved it, for all the lies.*
*As soon as she was done, she disappeared into the crowd,*
*No one could hear, because the music was loud*
*At home, she waited on the message.*
*Bereaved she cried, her lover died.*
*No one knows who shot him dead,*
*They think it's a man with a black hat.*
*Andromeda: "ruler of men" (meaning)*
*Took sweet revenge.*

# 45. Be Kind and Compassionate

*Be careful how you choose your words and tone of voice.*
*Encouraging someone is far better than putting them down.*
*Keep track of those who you know need an ear or maybe a prayer to hear.*
*Inspire them always with inspirational quotes or wise words.*
*Never surrender to giving up on someone who goes astray, just keep praying.*
*Dark days can happen to anyone, so if you can, be there for someone.*
*Always keep an open hand for giving and not just for receiving.*
*Never judge a book by its cover, we all need each other.*
*Do what you can for a friend who is in need, if it's your help they seek.*
*Check-in on those you did not hear from, to find how they do,*
*Often people don't want to burden you.*
*Make an effort to go visit someone who is sick or bereaved,*
*Perhaps your company and conversation are all they need.*
*Address everyone with respect and dignity,*
*Shows them we all deserve equality.*
*Smile when you greet a stranger, who knows in the future they might return the favor.*
*Invite a friend for a cup of tea or a walk at the beach,*
*Often it is all they need to break free from, the*
*Normally a routine of misery and pain.*
*Affection and compassion are good for the heart and brain.*

*Take some time also to spoil you,*
*Every one of us deserves a day to feel blue.*

# 46. Love Letter

*My dearest lover.*
*I wish we can still be together.*
*Every night, I watch the stars.*
*Wondering where you are.*
*Are you still in love with me?*
*Or happy to be free? Free from all the pain.*
*The tumor that drives you insane.*
*Do you miss me?*
*As I do.*
*How are you?*
*Can you see me from where you are?*
*When you soar above clouds. I still remember how you smell.*
*And all the silly jokes you used to tell.*
*I cry myself to sleep.*
*But grateful for your soul, God keeps.*
*I know you found peace.*
*And had to leave.*
*One day we will see each other.*
*My love for you,*
*Is stronger than ever.*
*Forever yours.*

# 47. Colored

*They say I am colored.*
*Can someone please explain?*
*What does it mean?*
*My blood is red like yours and theirs,*
*I might just have lighter or darker skin.*
*But what do I know, you are the expert.*
*I can converse with you.*
*I might have just a different accent.*
*But you can clearly understand*
*When I am talking.*
*But what do I know, you are the expert.*
*You say I am colored,*
*What makes me different?*
*Is it the texture of my hair?*
*Or the pigmentation of my skin?*
*I thought it just protects me from sunburn.*
*But what do I know, you are the expert.*
*What is colored? Do they look different?*
*Or like everyone, Blessed with more or less melanin?*
*But what do I know, you are the expert.*
*Are we all not colored?*
*Instead of white and black.*
*We all have different shades of hues.*
*Even you.*

*But what do I know, you are the expert.*

# 48. Until the next round

*When she looked at him,*
*She knows it is not just the room that is hot,*
*But her whole body is in heat.*
*He slowly undressed her,*
*His eyes penetrated her soul.*
*Teasing her body,*
*Filling her with hunger and desires.*
*How could such a Greek god*
*Choose her over all the beautiful women?*
*Blows still her mind.*
*His touch is gentle but also strong,*
*When he pulled her by her hair backward,*
*Passionately kiss her, all resistance crumbles.*
*Cooling her body by blowing his breath over it.*
*How could she not want more?*
*She literally begs him, with her moans.*
*Pleads to him not to stop.*
*She is dying inside for his touch.*
*Her hunger takes over,*
*She wants him to fill her up,*
*Gives her everything he got.*
*Taking her on the Ferris wheel,*
*Where she wants to stay on top.*
*High on adrenaline and testosterone,*

"

*Until they both cry out,*
*From passion and exhaustion.*
*Collapse down to earth.*
*Cuddling, Resting,*
*Until the next round.*

# 49. Undying love

*Tonight, at the foot of the bed,*
*She is watching.*
*How peaceful he is sleeping.*
*Wondering if he ever thought,*
*Of that crucial night,*
*That changed their lives?*
*He took off in a speed,*
*After revealing his secret.*
*Ended up in a hospital bed,*
*In need of a heart transplant.*
*Rushing to be with him,*
*Her life ended,*
*With a fatal accident.*
*Braindead, they said.*
*Now her heart is beating,*
*In his chest.*
*Feeling lost and betrayed,*
*She came to claim.*
*What is rightfully hers,*
*While he is sleeping,*
*.Next to his lover.*
*If she couldn't have him in the living,*
*While they both were alive.*
*Then it's time he must die.*

LET YOUR VOICE SPEAK

*They made their vows.*
*'Till death do us part.*

# 50. I want to go home

It is very dark and cold,
How had I ended up on this desolate road?
I still remembered packing my bags, I wanted to go home.
Now I am standing here alone,
Waiting for someone to give me a ride,
Why does every car pass me by?
And where is my phone?
I still remembered phoning home,
Talking to mum and dad,
Telling them, I will come home.
He does not want to stop with his affairs.
What am I doing on this road?
Why am I getting so very cold?
My head is throbbing very severe,
My heart is beating very slowly.
Why could nobody see me out here?
I am standing in the middle of the road,
With a heavy suitcase in my hand,
They can obviously see I am stranded.
Why could I not remember what happened?
After he enters the room.
Finding me packing my suitcase,
Telling him I am leaving.
I remembered he turned around, exiting the room.

*All I heard was a big bang and screaming.*
*What happened then?*
*I cannot remember anything. Mum and dad must be worried,*
*Wondering where I am. I want to go home, I don't want to be on this*
*road alone.*
*What are all these people doing out here?*
*Ambulance and police cars, looking for something.*
*Why don't they see me? Please I want to go home.*
*Mum, Dad, why are you here?*
*Not seeing me standing in front of you? Why are you two screaming and*
*crying? Whose body are they carrying?*
*Did they find it here, on this desolate road? Mum, dad I am here*
*I want to go home.*

# 51. Kaleidoscope

*The world is not always a rainbow.*
*From where I am standing.*
*Looking through my kaleidoscope.*
*I am observing, only black and grey*
*It is breaking my heart to see how many people,*
*Roaming my streets every day.*
*Scratching in bins for food,*
*Nothing to eat all day.*
*While the rich are sitting in fancy restaurants.*
*Just nibble on exotic food.*
*Drinking expensive wine.*
*Why could we not be more caring?*
*And share what we have.*
*After all, we all are children of God.*
*Looking through my kaleidoscope I see,*
*So many abuse their power.*
*Dedicated workers doing hard labor.*
*While managers sitting in air-con offices,*
*Doing nothing.*
*Why could we not be more caring?*
*And share equal responsibilities.*
*After all, we all are children of God.*
*Looking through my kaleidoscope, I only see black and grey.*
*When it comes to my government.*

*Stealing every day.*
*Pocket money from poor families.*
*Giving the scraps away.*
*How could they get away?*
*From stealing poor peoples' money.*
*After all, we all are children of God.*

# 52. The love of art

*If I use the sky as a canvas,*
*I like you to be my muse.*
*Different shades of colors, I can use.*
*You will be a masterpiece hanging in my gallery.*
*With your ebony curly hair,*
*Every maiden would drool to play.*
*Softly twirling their fingers around it, every day.*
*Your bright brown eyes will be mesmerized.*
*And capturing every lonely heart.*
*It would be really sad to walk away,*
*From such marvelous art.*
*A pointing nose that speaks of the aristocracy.*
*For you to behold righteousness, came easily.*
*A luscious soft pink mouth that screams,*
*For passionately kissing.*
*When it smiles, ladies weep,*
*For such a beautiful picture that weaken their knees.*
*A chocolate brownie body,*
*Forever ready to do, the mating dance.*
*How could such a sensual Adonis, Just be on a canvas.*
*Who knows the love of art.*

# 53. It is up to you

*Love is kind and gentle.*
*But also fierce and powerful.*
*Fighting for existence between,*
*Two people and millions.*
*It can unite or destroy, is*
*The line between hate and joy.*
*It speaks different languages in native tongues,*
*While expressing a thousand feelings,*
*Among old and young.*
*It cries when it is sad.*
*When deceived, crazy mad.*
*It is bereaved when someone dies.*
*And fill with joy for a baby's first cry.*
*Love is everywhere.*
*You don't need to seek to find it.*
*What type of love do you want to be?*
*Is up to you.*

# 54. How will I know?

*How does love feel?*
*Is it real?*
*How will I know?*
*I found love.*
*If I know nothing of,*
*The excitement you have,*
*Or the feelings you must share.*
*Is it refreshing like ice cream on a sunny day?*
*Or is it hot chocolate on a rainy May?*
*How is love?*
*Will you feel it in a touch?*
*When lips converse a message.*
*Or in the hugs?*
*Are you really on cloud nine?*
*When you say, I love you.*
*Does it mean, you are mine?*
*Is it necessary for bears, roses, and chocolates?*
*Why not a picnic in a park,*
*Watching the sunset before its dark?*
*How do you know it is love?*
*Will you see it in their eyes?*
*Or the way they smile.*
*Some say you feel butterflies.*
*And your emotions are high.*

*Am I in love?*

# 55. Love

*Somewhere love can still be found.*
*It is very rare but it can be shared.*
*It comforts a broken heart.*
*Consoling a troubled mind.*
*It bathes you with sunshine kisses on rainy days.*
*When tearing raindrops fall from your eyes.*
*And inside you softly cry.*
*Makes you feel completely safe.*
*When you are alone.*
*Thinking of your loved one at home.*
*Love whisper sweet endearments in your ears,*
*It takes away the uncertain fears.*
*Makes you hum a melody,*
*You like to hear it frequently.*
*It makes you silly and dizzy inside,*
*A feeling not easy to hide.*
*You smile from ear to ear,*
*Trusting it is for real.*
*A love that is gentle and kind,*
*Not playing games with your mind.*
*So when you fall again in love,*
*Knowing it is sent from heaven above*

# 56. Despicable me

*For using any obstacle.*
*They erect in my pathway.*
*As a pebble and not a mountain.*
*Despicable Me.*
*That I don't crumble.*
*In front of my frenemies.*
*But joyful singing.*
*They are anticipating,*
*Waiting to see if I am drowning.*
*But it is ok.*
*I have God in me.*
*They don't know on troubled water.*
*I prefer to dance gracefully.*
*Despicable Me.*
*For not competing.*
*With lies and deceit.*
*But undisturbed doing my work.*
*The eagle, in me, patiently waits.*
*The storm reached its peak.*
*Before I spread my majestic wings.*
*And when the dark clouds gather,*
*I am swiftly taking off.*
*And above the storm, I am soaring.*
*Become one with the roaring thunder,*

*And lightning.*
*Despicable Me.*
*For seeing.*
*With my optic eyes, far ahead*
*Their evil schemes.*
*Which was planned.*
*In their mind, they won.*
*But I have news for them.*
*A war had just begun.*
*I don't hail to no Caesar or Hitler.*
*But only to Jesus.*

# 57. Metamorphosis

*She is realizing now that,*
*Destiny had to take its course.*
*Her final stage of metamorphosis.*
*The caterpillar had to die,*
*To free the butterfly.*
*Her time has come.*
*To spread her wings and fly.*
*Negativity falling on deaf ears.*
*Embracing her life without fears.*
*Breaking free from all her insecurities,*
*Receiving with grace her blessings.*
*She has the wind under her wings,*
*Helping her to reach her dreams.*
*Sunrays bathing her face.*
*Giving her light for the darker days.*
*As fragile people think, she is,*
*She has a lioness personality.*
*The heroine of her story.*
*She slew dragons victoriously.*
*Bold and brave she can say,*
*I can face challenges any day.*

# 58. I am lost for words

*In the land of the blind,*
*There is always a one eye ruler.*
*Abuse her authority.*
*Being deceitful.*
*Even if it cost the kingdom,*
*And the people.*
*As long as she can rule with an iron fist.*
*Of course, she recruits an inner circle.*
*To help her with the dirty deeds.*
*In exchange for a few pennies.*
*And a seat at the table.*
*To enjoy the feast prepared by hard-working laborers.*
*They have no integrity.*
*But operate like a phony mafia.*
*I am lost for words*

# 59. Hello me

*I know you before your consummation happens.*
*I was already omnipresent waiting, for two bodies to conceive you.*
*I know who I will be and my destiny.*
*All I have to do is to wait for my season.*
*To be reborn from human spawn.*
*Waiting for the ovulation period.*
*And which sperm out of the millions,*
*Will be the victor.*
*Fighting to be first.*
*Quenched the ovum's thirst.*
*And when it is done, I'll come down,*
*From heaven claiming my body.*
*To experience life on Earth.*
*A human birth.*
*But I am only going to stay for a while,*
*Experience my journey.*
*To live eternally.*

# 60. Guardian Angel

*I had to fight with her today,*
*Made her understand she had to stay.*
*She cannot leave me alone,*
*Here on my own at home.*
*She is my inspiration,*
*My guardian angel.*
*Without her, I can't write nor all,*
*The battles I must fight.*
*I know if she open the door and go away,*
*I'll be on my own and astray.*
*She told me I am strong enough.*
*She is no more in need,*
*A new angel I will meet.*
*But I don't want someone else.*
*I need her, she is my mother.*
*Although she might not be here in flesh and bone,*
*But with her spirit around,*
*I feel not so alone.*

# 61. I am grateful

*My faith uphold me, for whom I am today,*
*A past that was not a bed of roses but full of pain.*
*During, my abusive years, I did not fear,*
*Because I knew my God was always near.*
*He protected me every time, even when I almost died.*
*Depression tried to corrupt my soul,*
*I stood firm, in faith and was bold.*
*In my darkest days, I received a vision.*
*From Daniel, a beautiful angel,*
*With a message, he protected me when I was in danger.*
*God heard all my prayers,*
*He was there when I was in despair.*
*Without faith, I would suffered from multiple addictions,*
*Especially when a monster ex-husband get us evicted.*
*On the streets I would have been with my kids.*
*But my faith kept me strong,*
*In front of Jesus' feet I hang on.*
*Now, I share my story to the world, using words of poetry.*

# 62. I am in trouble

*I have to go to jail,*
*For a crime I commit.*
*They said I refused to assist a dance enthusiast.*
*I would try to explain,*
*I did not want to refrain.*
*But my feet are bruised, you can see,*
*He struggled to keep the beat.*
*Every time I instructed him to go left,*
*He will go right.*
*Or forward, when we were supposed to go back.*
*With his big feet, he took the wrong steps,*
*Now he pursued a case against me,*
*Because I told him he has two left feet.*
*He said it is not fair,*
*Nobody wants him to dance anywhere*

# 63. I finally found me

*It took me years, to find me,*
*Whom I am, and what is my destiny.*
*I never fit in, around my friends and siblings,*
*Felt trap like a puppet on strings.*
*When I finally broke free from them all,*
*I immediately felt whole.*
*Being alone, feel never so pleasing,*
*I have time to do my writing.*
*I found a new me, inside,*
*Someone who broke free, who hide.*
*She found a purpose in life, in her poems,*
*She was finally free at home.*
*A new world open in front of me,*
*My soul had time to speak freely.*
*I could captured my words on a canvas,*
*Coloured it in with a beautiful verse.*
*I could inspired people like me,*
*Tell them about my life and abusive history.*
*I am a survivor due to poetry,*
*Completing my book is my destiny.*

# 64. A Love of a mother

*When I think of unconditional love, I think of my mother.*
*She did not just love her children, but everyone, especially God.*
*Her love could not be measured by any reward.*
*She would climbed the highest mountain,*
*Or swim the deepest ocean to safe her children.*
*Her love, I compare to a teardrop in the deep blue sea,*
*If you can find it, then she will stop loving me.*
*Although she is not with me anymore,*
*I still can feel her love that I adore.*
*My mothers' love is very rare,*
*But with everyone she had to share.*
*Unconditional Love is she, for truly loving me.*

# 65. Is family bound by blood?

*You can choose your friends, but not your family,*
*And I totally agreed.*
*But my friends are my family.*
*Bond by blood we may not be,*
*Brothers and sisters from different mothers everybody could see.*
*But we have more love and care,*
*Then most "real" families share.*
*They are daily in my prayers,*
*Sometimes we are in each other's affairs.*
*We fight like all siblings, over stupid things.*
*We laugh when we are happy,*
*And cry when someone dies.*
*Celebrates holidays, and birthdays together,*
*Promised to love each other forever.*
*Does it not make them my family too?*
*Or is it against society's rules?*
*I have a better relationship with them,*
*They are absolutely the best family-friends.*
*We may not share a bond of blood,*
*But amongst us we are the best family we got.*

# 66. Loyalty is unconditional love

*In her womb she protected and natured the most precious gem,*
*A promised she made to defend her baby's life until the end.*
*Many nights she lost so must sleep,*
*Safe her baby she must keep.*
*She watched you grow in a curious toddler,*
*Hoping that you will never forgot her.*
*As a teenager you gave her so much grief,*
*Her warnings you don't want to belief.*
*When you become an adult and moved out of the house,*
*Made you're a new life with a delinquent spouse.*
*She still promised you to keep you safe,*
*Even when your behaviour towards her had change.*
*She helped you raised your own baby,*
*Showed you still loyalty.*
*And when her time comes to say goodbye,*
*She held your hand, told you not to weep or cry.*

# 67. Magical seeds

*Hello friends, I am a pixie live in Fairyland,*
*Visiting everyday your homeland.*
*My pet is Grizelda as you can see,*
*She goes everywhere with me.*
*The two of us spread hope and kindness,*
*Precious gems that bind us.*
*We will only come when you in need,*
*Plant in your garden our magical seeds.*
*Every day we will watch how it grow,*
*In your behaviour it will show.*
*With fairy powder it will grow stronger,*
*Until it developed in an extraordinary flower.*
*When we see we had succeed,*
*We know it is time to leave.*
*Another human being is then in need,*
*To receive our precious seeds*

# 68. My midnight Dancer

*Sometimes when I go to bed, I have to dance with death.*
*It will always depends on his mood,*
*Which music will be good?*
*Now, before I lay down my head, I say a prayer in bed.*
*That tomorrow will be a new day, I will win the dance and,*
*Tonight will not be my last chance.*
*We will do the fox- trot or the tango,*
*The next morning my bedding will be tangled.*
*I prefer a quick step,*
*It's the only way to kick him off my bed.*
*We had once a slow waltz.*
*It put me in a trance.*
*That night, I was visited by black silhouettes,*
*They were waiting for me, surrounding my bed.*

# 69. The Curse

*It's not easy to be me,*
*I realized it now, even more.*
*I trust too soon,*
*Give people the benefit of the doubt.*
*End up hurting.*
*Betrayed by their nature,*
*I am like Alice in wonderland.*
*Chasing an imaginary friend.*
*I want to believe there is good in everyone.*
*But how could I?*
*You have more enemies than friends.*
*It sounds so cliché.*
*But it's true.*
*You are deceived by many.*
*Reached out a helping hand,*
*When they needed a friend.*
*To be stabbed in the back again.*
*Would I ever listen to my intuition?*
*I am the turtle, who trusts the scorpion.*
*It's hard to be an empath. If I don't understand me,*
*The curse I carry.*
*How could I expect, others too.*
*It is a fact.*
*I live in a world,*

ROEBAIN

*Where I am the fool. To trust is too easy.*

# 70. Embark the train

*Have you ever ponder on your past?*
*And realised it was mend to be.*
*You have the scars.*
*The wounds was the place,*
*For the light to come in.*
*Because of a sympathetic ear,*
*And what others' endured.*
*You are their train. Listen with empathy,*
*To their pain.*
*You know these friends,*
*Are passengers visiting an Inn.*
*They are just passing through.*
*Let them embark.*
*Listen to their hearts.*
*Give them quality advised.*
*They know you experienced it.*
*When they say goodbye.*
*You wished them well.*
*Another passenger is ready,*
*To embark the train.*

# 71. I am damaged

*I am not ready.*
*For a relationship.*
*Too damaged.*
*To have any.*
*I know now.*
*It will take a while,*
*To overcome my fears.*
*I found solitude.*
*I could,*
*Be myself.*
*Without worrying.*
*Be perfect,*
*Or be reject.*
*I found comfort,*
*In my soul.*
*That one day,*
*I will be whole.*
*Ready to try again,*
*Embracing a friend*

# 72. I

*I am me.*
*I am not what you perceived.*
*But*
*I am me*
*An African princess.*
*I am not a slave.*
*But I am me.*
*A daughter of a king.*
*I am not a victim.*
*But*
*I am me.*
*A victorious survivor.*
*I don't fear betrayers.*
*But I am me.*
*A brave heroine.*
*I don't listen to haters.*
*But*
*I am me.*
*I am a powerful human being*

# 73. My Ingenuity friend

*I miss you, yes you.*
*Where have you been?*
*Were you hiding or hibernating?*
*Your strong will and encouragement I seek,*
*Those inspired words you speak.*
*Always true to yourself,*
*Even if people gave you hell.*
*You stay cool, calm and collective,*
*Don't let cruel gossip be infectious.*
*Where have you been?*
*Did something unforeseen?*
*You don't let peoples' hate broke you down,*
*You make sure you stand your ground.*
*I know, their behavior caused sometimes pain,*
*You try to refrain, not think or react on it,*
*It makes you sick.*
*Don't worry my ingenuity friend,*
*The two of us will stay true friends.*
*You are my soul, and I am your body,*
*Together we ride our storms till the end.*

# 74. My moon friend

*At night she comes to say hello.*
*Adorned me with love and beauty.*
*Shining her soft, caresses light on her earth child.*
*Whisper sweet encouragement in my ears.*
*Shower me with sweet kisses on my cheeks,*
*Tell me her deep secrets.*
*Where she hide during daylight,*
*And about all the lovers that come at night.*
*How she wept for human kind.*
*When they are consumed with hate.*
*And how she prayed with those who lost their faith.*
*Her beauty never fades.*
*Even if she sometimes changes shape.*
*Remind us although we not always whole,*
*And go through different phases, we must never lose hope.*
*She will constantly watch us.*

# 75. The brave ones

*Ten poetesses decided to go on a quest.*
*To conquer the world not with a mighty sword,*
*But with a pen and their dangerous words.*
*Everywhere they go, the audience will file single rows.*
*To hear how they speak, their wisdom they seek.*
*One pulled an arrow out of a quiver.*
*Ready she released the string,*
*And with her words, the world blossoms into spring.*
*Another one pulled out a sword and wrote her words.*
*Amazed, before her eyes, everyone started to cry,*
*She wrote, "My father recently died."*
*Next was Jane, who pulled out a gun, shoot in the air,*
*I was betrayed by my ex-husband who had an affair.*
*And like the three before, all the others were adored.*
*For their wisdom they brought to an unholy world.*
*When they had to say goodbye,*
*Their audience cried every time.*
*Because unlike them, they were not so brave,*
*To speak out about their sorrows and pain.*

# 76. The Interview

*Waiting in line until it is my time.*
*I wondered what I will say,*
*What did I do, what is my excuse?*
*Looking apposite me, I am curious who she is.*
*She looks so pale and fragile.*
*I know she is dead from the blow in her head.*
*What life she had been living, by the clothes she wears,*
*And the blood dripping from her hair?*
*I bet she will bargain, to be pardoned.*
*The man next to me looks very conceited.*
*Bet he will plea that's not his fault he had a wealthy life,*
*Killed by his jealous wife.*
*It looks like he had an affair with the person in the other chair. Because*
*both are still naked,*
*With gunshots in their heads,*
*The reason their lives were terminated.*
*Still pondered what I will say, Why did I die on this day?*
*Mr. Peter, the gatekeeper looks so very stern, No regrets if he had to send*
*you to burn.*
*I don't think I have to say anything,*
*After all He knows my history and my abusive story.*
*As I look around and see these dreadful faces,*
*I know this interview is not based on gender, wealth or race.*
*You will be judged by the rules of the holy book,*

*It depends on what choices in life you took.*
*At last I heard my name,*
*Now my interview begins.*

# 77. The Promise

*All of herself, she gave,*
*Just to feel now betrayed.*
*Here, on the edge of the cliff, she sits,*
*Filled with emotions of regrets.*
*Every memory is tattooed on her body.*
*A promise was made, they will never separate.*
*How could he left her fragile and alone,*
*There is no one at home.*
*To whom must she share her stories and memories?*
*He is gone for good, laid in a box of wood.*
*If she could just turn the hands of time,*
*To tell him she changed her mind.*
*She would go with him to the farewell,*
*And not experienced this hell.*
*He would not drive back home, alone.*
*Still together they would be,*
*Instead of, in the deep blue sea.*
*Now, she had to scatter his ashes,*
*Where it happened, and threw herself down.*
*A promise was made, this is her fate.*

# 78. The journey

*When the puppeteer finished his last product,*
*He was sending them out.*
*With these words,*
*"Go out and fulfill your dreams*
*And make me proud.*
*I will call you one day.*
*To return and ask you,*
*How was your journey?"*
*The first who one was made was asking,*
*Do I have to go?*
*In this big world?*
*I would prefer to stay with you.*
*"No, my dear everyone had to go, finding their specialty*
*Even you, who was with me since the beginning."*
*After many seasons, He called them back.*
*And as promised,*
*They all returned.*
*The puppeteer was asking,*
*"My dear ones, what have you learned?"*
*Many answers were the same.*
*They see a world full of splendor,*
*They made people laugh with their,*
*Jumping, singing, and dancing on their strings.*
*The last puppet who wanted to stay,*

*Was asked to tell his story.*
*I see a world where people are the puppets,*
*Controlled by a minority.*
*There is no respect for individuality.*
*You have to do and say,*
*As you were commanding.*
*I refused to obey their rules,*
*And uphold my values and integrity.*
*Because you told me we have only one master.*
*The master was smiling and nodding his head,*
*"At least one was listening and enjoying the journey*

# 79. Escape

*I have to escape,*
*Sometimes from an insanity mundane lifestyle.*
*And just do me.*
*Finding a quiet place,*
*Where I can read and write poetry.*
*If I could, I would leave,*
*All this behind,*
*And find a place where humans are sane.*
*Living a simple life,*
*Where equality speaks.*
*And everybody lives in harmony.*
*Where the lion and lamb are friends.*
*Respecting each other,*
*As sister and brother.*
*Where dreams are real.*
*And wishes come true.*

# 80. Shadow

*There is a shadow that follows you and me.*
*Since we were babies.*
*It grows stronger as we become adults.*
*This shadow creeps upon us,*
*Unexpectedly like obesity.*
*You only realized what it is,*
*When you lost dearly.*
*It divides friends and family,*
*And creates animosity between,*
*Nations and countries.*
*As it manifests on you, it grows,*
*You become weaker and lose self-control.*
*So be careful of your shadow,*
*It will hate you.*
*When it devours your soul*

# 81. Live under one umbrella

*Humanity is you and me, living together in harmony.*
*Showing kindness and respect are some virtues of Ubuntu.*
*Reaching out with a helping hand, not only to family and friends,*
*But especially to strangers and our neighbours, it shows solidarity and*
*co-responsibility.*
*is my child, so if you need help,*
*Please, be free and ask me.*
*Live under the code, your child*
*It teaches us to co-exist no matter religion or colour,*
*We are after all, sisters and brothers.*
*Forget about diversity, we should live free,*
*Under the same sun and not killing each other with guns.*
*Morality, acceptance and communality, are principles of humanity.*
*But it's our responsibility to make sure we adhere, spread peace and not*
*fear, everywhere.*
*To share our world together under one umbrella.*

# 82. Dry your tears

*As I am sitting on the top of the mountain,*
*Wondering will I ever fit anywhere in.*
*A heart filled with pain.*
*Your soul is in despair.*
*Because love slip out of your hands,*
*Time, and time again.*
*Suddenly a mighty voice is speaking.*
*"My child, do you really think this world belongs to you and me?"*
*I might have created it many years ago.*
*But soon I will come and take you home.*
*You are only visiting for a while,*
*Being an earthly guess.*
*Soon you will close your eyes,*
*While your body will be put to rest.*
*But the good news is,*
*Where I am taking you, life begins.*
*No more pain and suffering,*
*But a life filled with endless love.*
*A pretty rose in my garden you will be.*
*Blossoming eternally.*
*Dry your tears my precious gem,*
*I am here.*
*Hold on to my promise dear.*
*No more heartache and pain,*

*But blessings, abundantly.*

# 83. Love is a rose

*If love is a rose, it has beauty, multiple layers of humanity.*
*Fragrances that draw you near, a scent that will not disappear.*
*Every petal has a unique quality, speaks to the heart frequently.*
*Words of, kindness, compassion, and honesty, keep you captivating and*
*interesting.*
*Every dewdrop is a tear of joy, peace, and its' leaves, the embracing*
*feeling,*
*of safety.*
*Protect with thorns to warn, thee not to hurt, but adore you.*

# 84. Innocence

*Look into my eyes.*
*What do you see?*
*It's only me,*
*Who perceived the world differently?*
*Not black and grey,*
*But pure white as snow.*
*I still believe in fairies,*
*Dragons and unicorns.*
*A leprechaun with a pot of gold,*
*At the other side of the rainbow.*
*So why do you show me,*
*Things I don't want to see?*
*Abused, naked women on a bed,*
*Bodies beaten to dead.*
*Humans killing each other.*
*With weapons and drugs,*
*Half naked women dancing with thugs.*
*Please, keep my innocence,*
*Let me remain a child.*
*I have plenty of time,*
*To grow and adapt in the wild.*

# 85. Real men don't

*12 years ago,*
*On the first day,*
*Of the16 day campaign.*
*My life was nearly ending.*
*By the hand of a brutal man.*
*God saved me.*
*I am grateful.*
*Having more time with my kids.*
*Not all women are privileged.*
*It's that time of the year again,*
*To campaign.*
*Against women and child abuse.*
*Only 16 days for women to have rights.*
*To speak up.*
*This is not enough.*
*What about all the other days of the year?*
*We have to live in fear.*
*Ironically, during these days.*
*More women are killed or raped.*
*Narcissistic men do their deeds*
*With a bullet or knife,*
*End a woman's life.*
*Rape victims are too scared,*
*To speak out.*

*Afraid to get labeled.*
*What will the prosecutor or media say?*
*"Her skirt was too short,*
*Her body reveals too much.*
*The courses of his lust."*
*I like to ask these men,*
*Do you have a mum?*
*Sister, wife, or daughter at home?*
*Will, it is ok if,*
*Do they get killed or raped?*

# 86. Jasmine

*Jasmine was an innocent soul.*
*Who married a narcissistic pig.*
*After three months she was pregnant.*
*The news was embraced with a brick in her face.*
*He did not sign up for that.*
*He was not ready to be a dad.*
*He wanted his freedom.*
*Drink and have parties with his friends.*
*She endured the violence.*
*Kept silent.*
*A second baby was on the way.*
*But that did not stop the pain.*
*His rage got even worse.*
*She wanted to file for a divorce.*
*He made her scared,*
*Promised her death.*
*After years of abuse.*
*She devised an escape plan.*
*On a dark, stormy night,*
*She grabbed the kids and ran away.*
*But to all dismay,*
*A drunk driver did a hit and run.*
*Three lives end.*

# 87. What will you do?

*Women,*
*Can you hear it too?*
*The pulsating of your lovers' hearts.*
*When it beats fast,*
*Then it normally should.*
*Pumping with endorphins.*
*Testosterone is kicking in.*
*The body is high on adrenaline.*
*Women what do you think,*
*Should you rescue him?*
*Slow down his heart rate.*
*Or leave him to his fate?*
*Or should you?*
*Give him some ecstasy,*
*Take him out of his misery.*
*Or would you?*
*Dress up and go out.*
*With your girlfriends.*
*Have some fun,*
*The night is still young.*

# 88. Rumours

*I have a bone to pick with you.*
*I heard you spread rumours about me.*
*Said, I am courageous,*
*And have endurance.*
*Am very smart,*
*Have a good heart.*
*You like my smile,*
*The sparkling in my eyes.*
*Are they true?*
*Was it you?*
*Or are these rumours all lies?*
*I'd like to hear,*
*From your mouth to my ear.*
*So I could spread rumours about you too.*

# 89. Hambe kahle

*Hamba Kahle my dear friend.*
*I wish we had more time,*
*To use the wind and sail,*
*Across the seven seas.*
*Or spread our wings and fly,*
*Explore all our beautiful dreams.*
*But God knows why.*
*And when it is our time.*
*So please be my guide,*
*As you step into the light.*
*Keep an eye on me.*
*I know I will feel,*
*Your presence near,*
*When the wind plays with my hair.*
*Goodbye, I promise not to cry.*

# 90. Truth

There are three things in life,
That cannot hide.
The sun, moon and truth.
Sometimes the truth is hidden,
In a black hole.
Covered up by lies.
But when the light is shining,
Where darkness is hiding,
Truth is revealed.
Shadows lurking around,
A new soul they want.
Be careful who you trust.
Lies can be covered up.
If eyes reveals the soul,
Then truth will be told,
By looking into them.
Before you trust a friend.
The enemy is not always,
Unknown.
Truth cannot hide for long.
So look into their eyes
It will reveal their lies.

# 91. The wild

*When I say I am from South Africa.*
*People usually ask me,*
*Does the wild live amongst you?*
*I would smile, and say,*
*Yes, they do.*
*They are roaming the streets every day.*
*But the secret is,*
*They look like you and me.*
*Our murderers, rapists, drug lords,*
*and pedophiles.*
*They are just camouflaged.*
*Hiding behind their devilish smiles.*
*They act like human beings.*
*The only difference is,*
*They have hearts as black as coal.*
*And only one goal.*
*To hurt other people.*
*They are roaming in a manmade jungle.*
*Growing each day, in numbers.*
*Because they sold their souls.*
*For wealth and power.*
*It takes courage to tame them.*

# 92. My prayer

*Sometimes you revisit the past.*
*To make sense of the lessons,*
*You learned.*
*To have the courage to face the truth.*
*That the world was not ready yet,*
*For you.*
*All the gifts that you can offer.*
*Everyone has their own season,*
*To blossom.*
*Flowers don't compete,*
*With each other.*
*But embracing all beauty.*
*Nature lives in harmony.*
*So why couldn't we?*
*Always full of deceit and lies,*
*Ready to grab the first price.*
*If we only,*
*Appreciate life instead,*
*Of wealth.*
*We can live in love and peace.*
*This is my prayer for us.*

# 93. The pact

*What will you do, when a man tells you,*
*After 20 years he never loves you?*
*He wishes you dead.*
*He only married you for the benefits.*
*What will you do?*
*I made a pact.*
*The pain I endured,*
*I'll never feel it again.*
*I had to cut all the poison,*
*From every cell and vein,*
*Out of my body and memory.*
*It took a while to recover,*
*And heal from a scorpions' sting,*
*But luckily I have God and my kids.*
*His poison kept me in prison,*
*For many years.*
*I build a wall around myself,*
*To fall in love never again.*
*But then I realized,*
*If I let this wall, just get stronger,*
*He will win.*
*I remain a victim.*
*I took a sledgehammer,*
*And broke it down.*

*I am free,*
*No more a captive,*
*But a survivor.*

# 94. Patriot

*When I get the opportunity,*
*To travel*
*I choose my country.*
*It was here I was born.*
*My mum gave birth to me at home.*
*My ancestors walk on this land.*
*Build buildings with their bare hands.*
*As a child I played amongst the fauna and flora.*
*Learning to appreciate culture and diversity.*
*Growing up during the segregation laws.*
*But still we have Ubuntu in us.*
*There is so much beauty to see.*
*In spite all the negativities.*
*I am my country.*
*And my country is me.*

# 95. It was not easy

*I finished the climb, victory is finally mine!*
*At the foot of the mountain, its seemed endless high,*
*Now, I am standing tall,*
*I won an emotional war.*
*I broke free, from a terrible past,*
*That I thought would forever last.*
*Here, I am God, on your mountain,*
*Your mercies and grace overflow me like a fountain.*
*I raised, my hands and head to You,*
*Because of Your love, my life continues.*
*Finally, I can breathe fresh air, not suffocated without breath,*
*Choked on death.*
*I am free, like an eagle.*
*I want to soar high from this mountain.*
*High, high in the sky.*
*To reach the top was not easy.*
*But it is an amazing feeling.*
*I gave up a lot to be free,*
*Now I am surrounded with peace in me.*

# 96. God will intervene

*On the top of Table mountain, I am standing.*
*Raising my head, inhaling a deep breath,*
*of fresh air .*
*Enjoying the sun rays on my face,*
*Before I am spreading my wings.*
*I have so much admiration for nature,*
*with all Gods' splendor.*
*High, green tree tops pointing to the blue sky,*
*While swallows and crows fly gracefully.*
*And underneath, dassies carefree playing.*
*I flap my wings and start to fly.*
*High, high above the mountain and trees.*
*Diving down to the city,*
*Where I see homeless people, roaming the streets.*
*Scratching in bins for something to eat.*
*Tears of sadness falling from my eyes, inside I cry.*
*Because some of us are lost.*
*No more humanity, as long they are rich.*
*They don't care about the poor and their dignity.*
*I wish at the moment I could help them all,*
*But I know it is impossible.*
*Instead I am folding my wings, praying.*
*God will intervene.*

# 97. A walk to freedom

*The sky is the limit for me.*
*I am breaking free,*
*From all the boundaries.*
*Now I have a universe to explore.*
*After I closed the door.*
*Every day is a leap of faith.*
*Knowing, I will make mistakes.*
*One tiny step makes a huge impact.*
*Where I was and heading.*
*Friends and family are my stepping stones.*
*Along my walk to freedom.*
*I have no regrets for who I am.*
*My life is in God's hands.*
*Obstacles might come on the path.*
*I would not allow it to tear me apart.*
*I will walk in green pastures from now on.*
*A long walk for freedom.*

# 98. Sipping on an exotic drink

*All mums are superheroes,*
*Yes, we know.*
*We have four eyes, arms, and legs.*
*Keeping everybody happy,*
*And listen to all the complains,*
*Giving solutions to your problems.*
*But sometimes superheroes,*
*Also need a break from reality.*
*And she wants to go on holiday.*
*Laying lazy on a hammock,*
*Sipping on an exotic drink.*
*While a soft breeze plays with,*
*Her grey hair.*
*And sunrays kisses, soothes her wrinkled skin.*
*With her eyes closed, she listens to the whispering*
*Of the wind, singing her a special melody.*
*For all those times she felt so lonely.*
*When she had to play nurse until late at night.*
*Or an attorney, when her child was bullied.*
*Domestic worker, cleaning up behind everyone,*
*Teacher to figure out what is one plus one.*
*For all those times, she was fighting against,*
*The monsters that want to destroy a happy home.*
*Or the times she was crying alone.*

*Hiding where no one can see,*
*She is not that strong.*
*So next time mum sounds crazy,*
*Humming out of tune.*
*Then she lays lazy on her hammock,*
*Sipping on an exotic drink.*

# 99. Be an Inspiration

*Believing in yourself is the best thing to do, to reach for your dreams,*
*Even if it seems nothing goes your way, don't give up, you will not fail.*
*Accomplishments take time to achieve, as long as you reach for the stars*
*and believe.*
*Never doubt yourself and give in to fears, close your ears for negative*
*criticism you hear.*
*Involve you in projects that can make your dreams come true, although*
*you think it might not be for you.*
*Negative thoughts will come and go, the secret is to keep them under*
*control.*
*Stay focused on what is your end goal,*
*Peer pressure can play a role, but you have to be strong and bold.*
*Individuality is the key to success, sometimes not all your friends you*
*would be able to keep.*
*Reach out for a helping hand but be careful not everybody is our friend.*
*Affirm every accomplishment you want to do, don't let past failures keep*
*you blue.*
*To be true to yourself is the best quality, it makes everything a possibility.*
*Introspection sometimes is very good, it gives clearance to what keeps you*
*in the loop.*
*Observe what is new and working for you and throw the old ones away.*
*Now go grab those aspirations because you are equipped with all the*
*inspirations.*

# 100. She is ready

*Majestic and powerful she feels, standing next to her King.*
*Both are ready for whatever their enemy is planning.*
*Today is her day, for showing them who her alliance is.*
*Greater is He who always was and will be,*
*Then those whose alliance is with the beast.*
*Her mood is calm, and her mind sharp.*
*Patience is her virtue,*
*Today her arrows will speak the truth.*
*She is in no need of an army, to win the war,*
*All she needs is her God.*
*He is the King of all kings,*
*Many battles, He wins.*
*On top of the mountain, He will show them,*
*His roar is louder than thunder.*
*And His eyes are brighter than the sun.*
*With speed faster than lightning.*
*And claws sharper than blades.*
*In Him, she puts all her faith.*
*Their biggest mistake they made,*
*Is to underestimate the power of her King*